EVERYDAY STEM

WAVES

Cheryl Mansfield and John Willis

AV2

www.av2books.com

Step 1
Go to **www.av2books.com**

Step 2
Enter this unique code
NAEBMMW5H

Step 3
Explore your interactive eBook!

AV2 is optimized for use on any device

Your interactive eBook comes with...

Contents
Browse a live contents page to easily navigate through resources

Audio
Listen to sections of the book read aloud

Videos
Watch informative video clips

Weblinks
Gain additional information for research

Try This!
Complete activities and hands-on experiments

Key Words
Study vocabulary, and complete a matching word activity

Quizzes
Test your knowledge

Slideshows
View images and captions

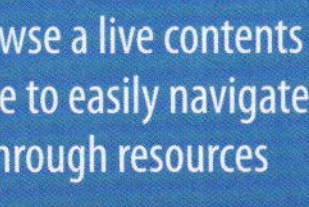

... and much, much more!

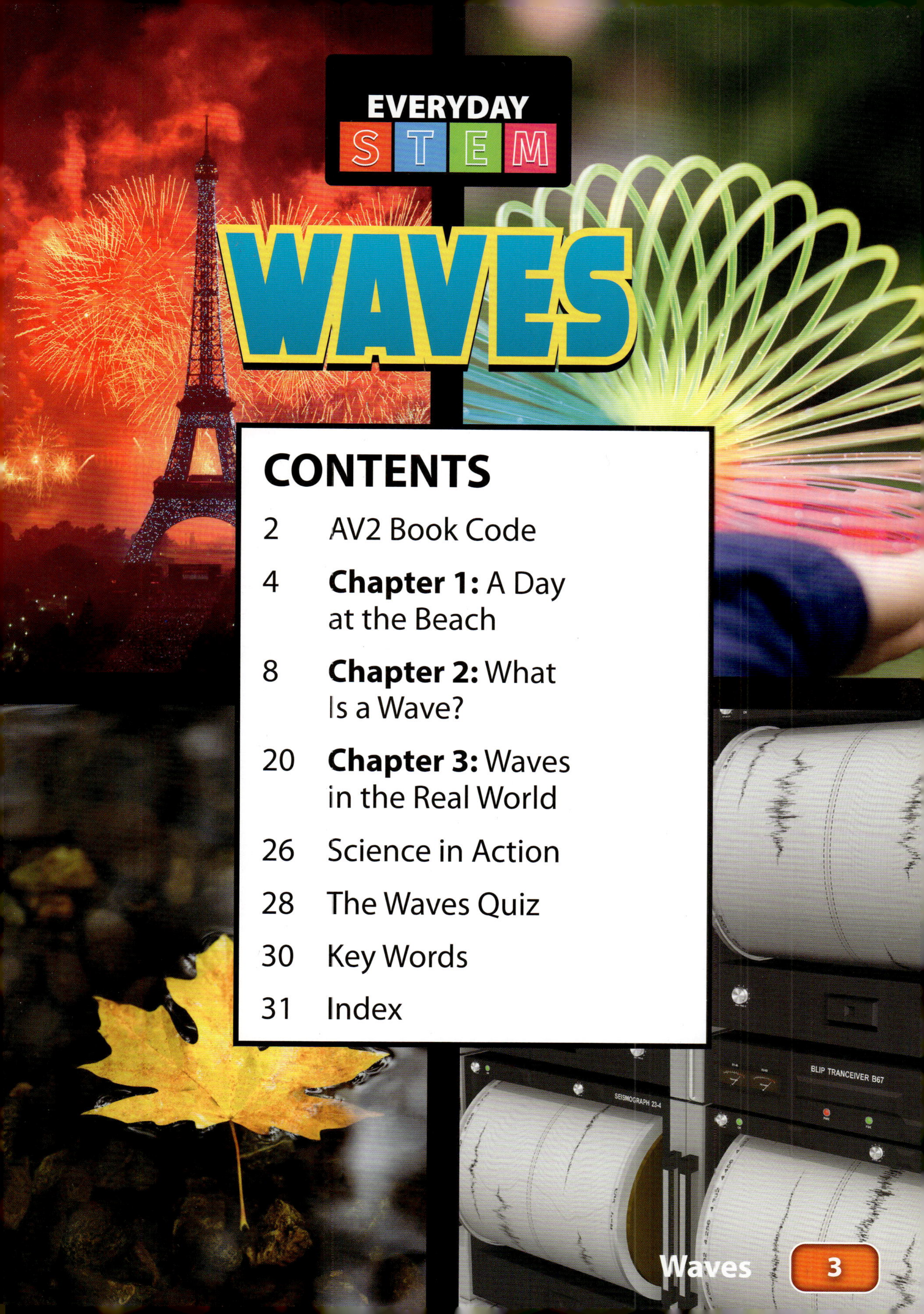

CONTENTS

CHAPTER ONE

A Day at the Beach

Heidi is at the beach with her family. She runs to the shore. A small wave rolls onto her feet. Then she looks out at the ocean. She sees surfers riding large waves. What causes these waves to happen?

Waves are regular **patterns** of motion. They are caused when an energy source creates a **disturbance**. This disturbance then travels. It carries energy from one place to another.

For waves on a lake, the energy source is usually the wind. The ripples on the surface are the disturbance. The disturbance carries the energy of the wave.

But waves are not only in water. They are everywhere in nature.

Waves created by the wind are also known as surface waves.

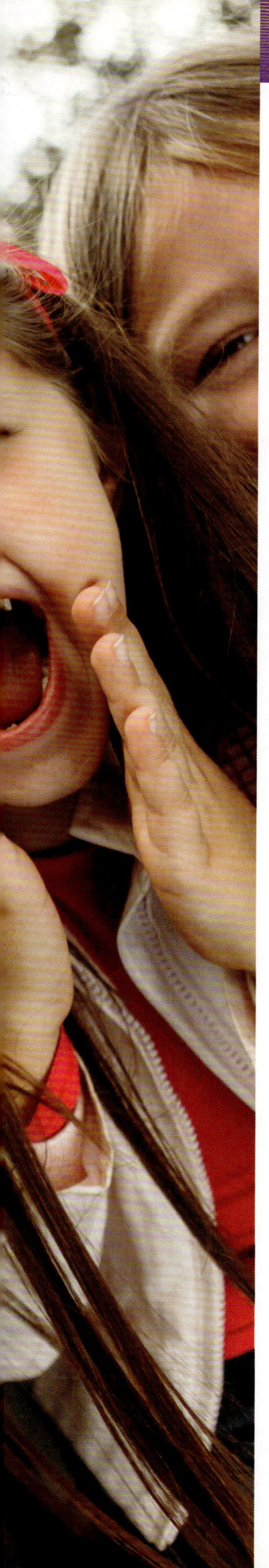

CHAPTER TWO

What Is a Wave?

There are many types of waves in nature. One type is called mechanical waves. Another type is called electromagnetic waves.

Mechanical waves need the help of **matter** to make them move. Particles in matter bump into other particles. Energy is passed between particles as the wave travels. Ocean waves are one example of mechanical waves. Sound waves are another.

Light waves that can be seen by human eyes are known as visible light.

Electromagnetic waves are different from mechanical waves. They can travel without the help of matter. They can travel through space. Radio waves are one example of electromagnetic waves. Light waves are another example.

For example, electromagnetic waves from the Sun travel through space. They reach Earth even though there is very little matter in space.

Waves move in different ways. Some waves are known as transverse waves. In these waves, the wave travels in one direction. However, the disturbance moves back and forth in a **perpendicular** direction. For example, suppose a transverse wave is traveling upward. The disturbance moves back and forth **horizontally**. Electromagnetic waves are one example of transverse waves.

Some waves move another way. In longitudinal waves, the disturbance moves back and forth in the same direction that the wave travels. Sound waves are an example. These waves travel through the air. They allow us to hear.

TRANSVERSE AND LONGITUDINAL WAVES

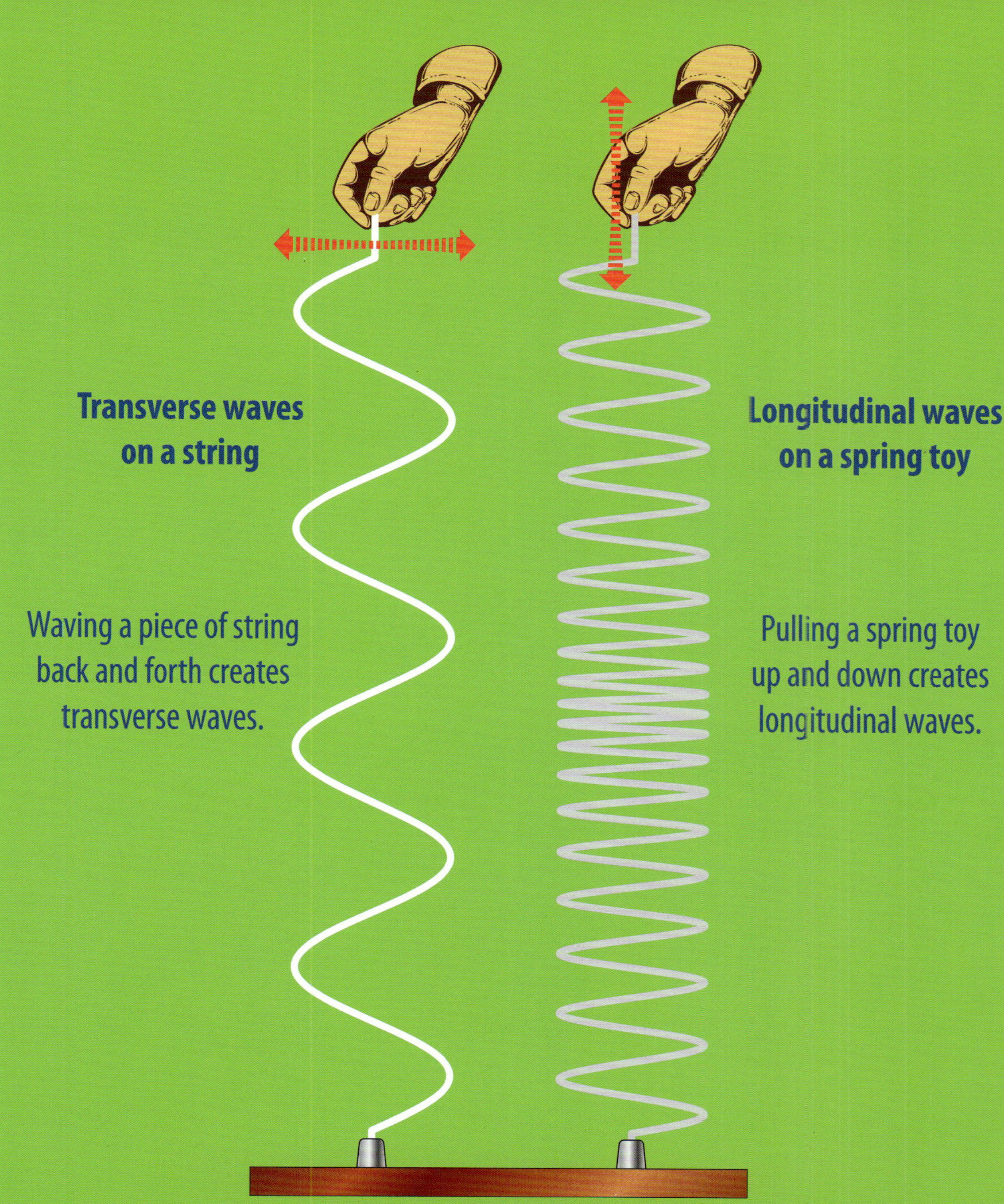

Ripples that move a leaf in a pond are a gentle form of wave.

Water waves are more complicated. They involve both transverse and longitudinal motion. Imagine a leaf floating on the surface of a pond. When a wave passes by, the leaf moves up and down. It also moves side to side.

Scientists measure waves in different ways. One measurement is called amplitude. This measures how large the disturbance is. The amplitude of a wave is related to the wave's energy.

Storm ocean waves crash into land with high energy.

For water waves, the top of the wave is called the crest. The bottom of the wave is called the trough. The amplitude measures how high the crest is compared to the water level. The amplitude also measures how low the trough is.

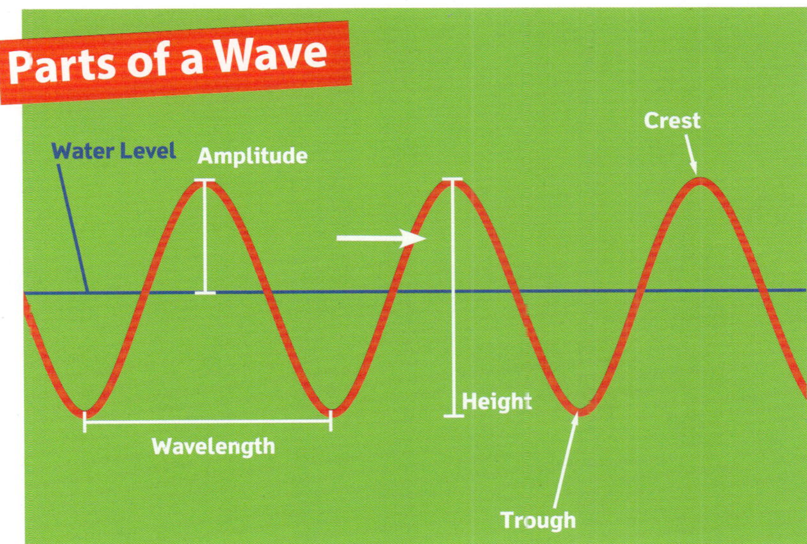

Some waves have low energy, such as small ripples on a pond. Other waves have high energy, such as large waves on the ocean.

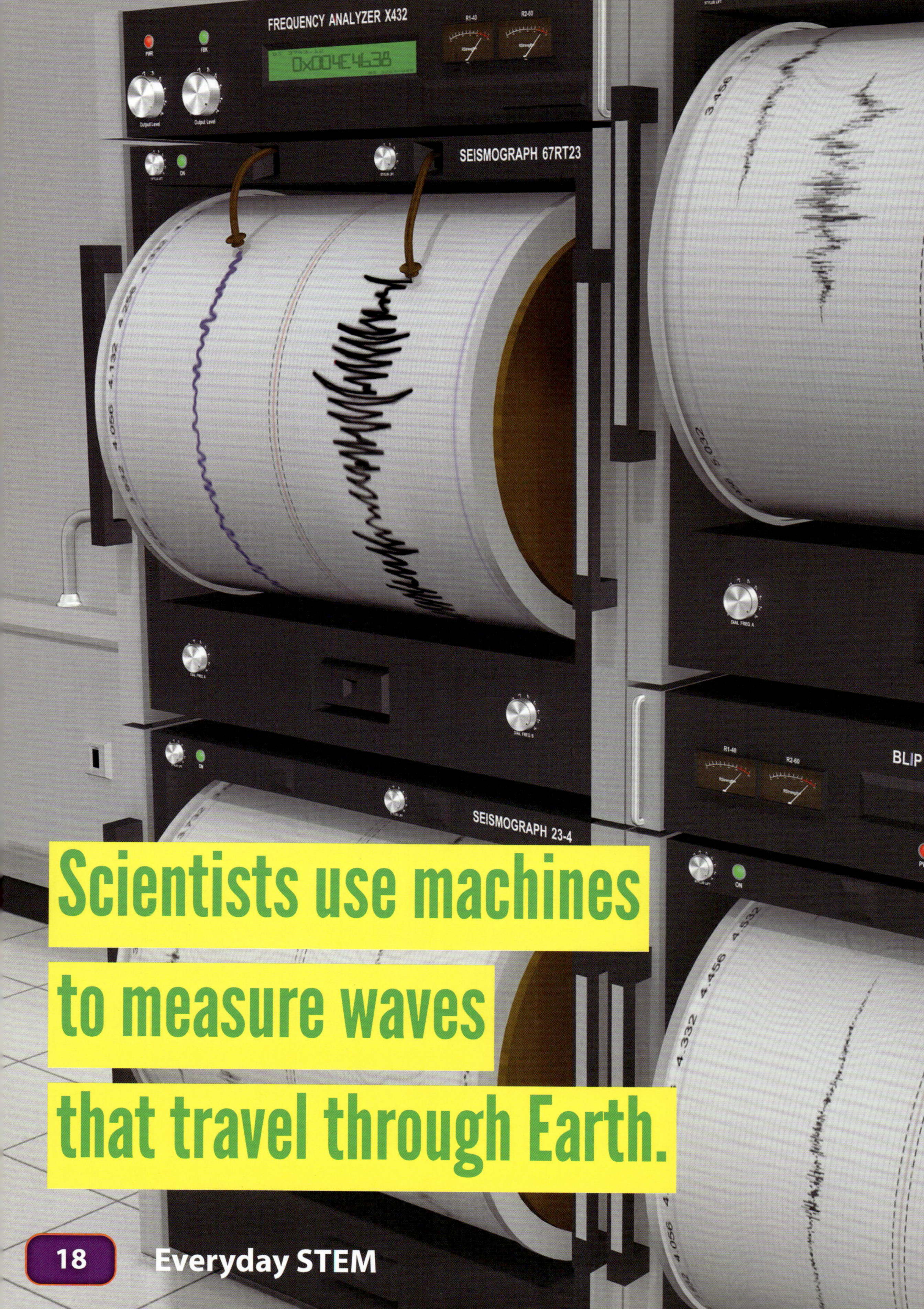

Scientists use machines to measure waves that travel through Earth.

Wavelength is another measurement. It tells the length of one complete cycle of a wave. Some waves have tiny wavelengths. For example, X-rays can have wavelengths that are smaller than the width of an **atom**. Other waves have huge wavelengths. Radio waves can have wavelengths that are longer than a football field.

Scientists can also measure a wave's period, frequency, and speed. The period of a wave is the amount of time it takes to complete one cycle. The frequency is the number of cycles passing by a point every second. The speed of the wave is how fast it travels.

CHAPTER THREE

Waves in the Real World

Waves are all around us. Many of them are helpful, but some can be harmful. Earthquakes involve waves inside Earth. These waves cause the ground to tremble. This can destroy buildings. Tsunamis can be harmful, too. These huge ocean waves can cause major damage.

Satellites send information around the world using electromagnetic waves.

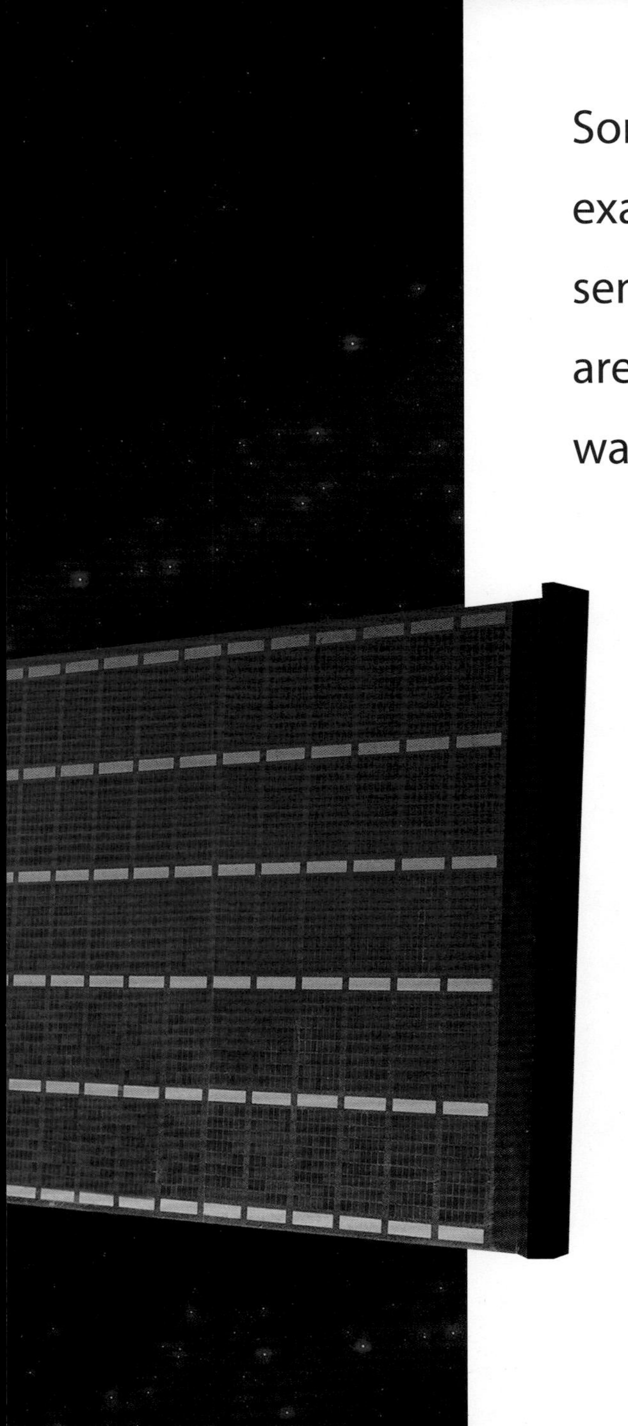

Some waves are very useful. For example, we use radio waves to send information. These waves are a type of electromagnetic wave. They are used in cell phones and TVs. They are used with **satellites**, too.

People also use waves to cook. Microwaves are another type of electromagnetic wave. The waves in a microwave oven heat the water in food. This causes the food to get warmer.

Waves are important in hospitals, too. For example, doctors use X-rays. This is another type of electromagnetic wave. X-rays can pass easily through skin but not very easily through bone. X-rays let doctors see inside our bodies.

Without waves, we would not be able to see. Light waves bounce off objects. Then the waves go into our eyes. This allows us to see. We use waves every day!

Light waves allow people to read words printed on a page.

Science in Action

Make Waves with a Spring Toy

Can you make waves with a spring toy? Perform this experiment to find out.

Ask a friend to hold one end of the spring toy on the floor. Keep it still.

Hold the other end of the spring toy in your hand. Make sure it is directly above the bottom end.

STEP 3

Quickly move your end of the spring toy left and right. In which direction do the waves move? Are these waves transverse or longitudinal? How could you make the other type of wave?

THE WAVES QUIZ

- 1 -

What causes a wave?

A. An energy source creates a disturbance

- 2 -

What is the usual source for waves on a lake?

A. The wind

- 3 -

What are two types of mechanical waves?

A. Ocean waves and sound waves

- 4 -

Does a wave carry energy from one place to another?

A. Yes

- 5 -

What type of waves travel through a spring toy?

A. Longitudinal waves

- 6 -

Can electromagnetic waves travel through space?

A. Yes

- 7 -

What are the top and bottom of a wave called?

A. Crest, trough

- 8 -

What waves are used to see inside the body?

A. X-rays

- 9 -

What machine uses waves to cook food?

A. A microwave oven

- 10 -

How do waves help us see?

A. Light waves bounce off objects

Key Words

atom: a small unit of matter that most of the objects around us are made of

disturbance: the thing that carries energy as a wave travels

horizontally: in a way that is parallel to the ground

matter: anything that takes up space

patterns: things that repeat regularly

perpendicular: at a 90-degree angle with another surface

satellites: objects in space that travel around much larger objects

Index

Get the best of both worlds.

AV2 bridges the gap between print and digital.

The expandable resources toolbar enables quick access to content including **videos**, **audio**, **activities**, **weblinks**, **slideshows**, **quizzes**, and **key words**.

Animated videos make static images come alive.

Resource icons on each page help readers to further **explore key concepts**.

Published by AV2
14 Penn Plaza, 9th Floor New York, NY 10122
Website: www.av2books.com

Library of Congress Control Number: 2020936970

ISBN 978-1-7911-2392-5 (hardcover)
ISBN 978-1-7911-2393-2 (softcover)
ISBN 978-1-7911-2394-9 (multi-user eBook)
ISBN 978-1-7911-2395-6 (single-user eBook)

Printed in Guangzhou, China
1 2 3 4 5 6 7 8 9 0 24 23 22 21 20

052020
101319

Designer: Terry Paulhus Project Coordinator: Priyanka Das

The publisher acknowledges Getty Images, iStock, and Shutterstock as its primary image suppliers for this title.

First published by Focus Readers in 2018.